A LOT ALIKE

WHAT EVERY ENTREPRENEUR SHOULD KNOW ABOUT BRANDING AND PURPOSE

MARANDA JOINER

Copyright © 2021 by Maranda Joiner

A Lot Alike: What Every Entrepreneur Should Know About Branding & Purpose

ALL RIGHTS RESERVED. No part of this publication may be reproduced, stored in a retrieval system, or transmitted in any form or by any means, electronic, mechanical, photocopying, recording or otherwise without the prior permission of the publisher or in accordance with the provisions of the Copyright, Designs, and Patents Act 1988 or under the terms of any license permitting limited copying issued by the Copyright Licensing Agency. The views expressed in this work are solely those of the author and do not necessarily reflect the views of the publisher, the publisher hereby disclaims any responsibility for them.

Cover Design: Rob Benson Design
Photo Credit: Bryan Mckenny
Illustrations: Picture It Possible
Content Editor: Chris Kelly Ink
Book layout and design: SISU Creative Studio

ISBN: 978-1-7367695-0-8

Printed in the United States of America

TABLE OF CONTENTS

Dedication | 4

Introduction: If You're Looking for Purpose, Turn Around | 6

Part One: (In the Beginning, There Was Branding)

Chapter One: Finding Purpose in Your Past | 15

Chapter Two: Your Target Audience Has a Name | 27

Chapter Three: Dream Big | 37

Part Two: (In the Middle There Was Organization)

Chapter Four: The Elevator Pitch | 43

Chapter Five: A Mission Statement You Can Feel | 51

Chapter Six: Get Out of Your Feelings | 59

Part Three: (Marketing is Just the Beginning)

Chapter Seven: How to Court and Date Your Audience | 67

Chapter Eight: The Wide, Wide World of Social Media | 79

Chapter Nine: Failure Has Fooled Us All | 93

My Random Final Thoughts | 101

Visual Mapping | 103

Notes Section | 105

About the Author | 114

DEDICATION

I dedicate this book to every entrepreneur that walked away from a thankless job that didn't align with their purpose. To every entrepreneur that has ever felt alone or lost in their journey. To every badass that had the strength to believe in that still small voice on the inside telling them to keep going. My hope is that this book will be a part of your story, leading you down the road of success to clarity, connection and financial freedom.

I want to thank my son Daniel for being such an amazing soul. Thank you for never making me feel guilty about all the hours I've spent as an entrepreneur and the time invested in bringing this book to life. Mom guilt is real but I promise it will be worth it in the long run. My hope is that you will see what it takes to dream big and push past fear to live life with no limitations. You can do anything you put your mind to.

To Kristin, my project manager who was as dedicated

and committed to seeing this book come to life as I was. It would not have come together as seamlessly and as quickly as it did, had it not been for your help. Thank you. To the top.

And to every friend, follower, and supporter; I wrote this book with you in mind. No lie, I wrote and read back over each chapter and thought about how it would make your life better. I hope I come close to the impact that I imagined it to have. Love you all.

INTRODUCTION

"Lean into the microphone and pretend like it's your boyfriend's ear." These were the last words I heard as the producer closed the production room door behind me.

Before I can explain what's happening here, we have to go back to my last semester in college. I was set to graduate from Belhaven College in the fall of 2003. Everything was in place except for one thing – a missing class required for graduation. I was left with two choices; drop out or pay another $8,000 to take it.

The balance of my bank account was telling me to cut my losses, but I decided to get it done anyway. After all, I had come this far. As frustrated as I was at the extended stay in school, much to my surprise, it turned out to be the semester that I landed an internship at the number one Hip Hop station in Jackson, Mississippi. I grew up listening to Alice Marie, Sam Brown, and DJ Finesse on WJMI right along with Stan Branson and Lady V on

KIXIE. Hell, it was the station my mother grew up listening to, so needless to say, I was more than a little excited to have a foot in the door.

The station didn't hire many interns, so I wasn't sure which magical unicorn had farted and landed me the privilege of being one of the few. But alas, there I was part of a crew who had worked there for years. It truly felt like the clouds had parted in my favor.

As an intern, I did the basic things that interns are tasked with: office work, filing, making copies, and shadowing the sales team. I never actually got close to the on-air mics. At least not until the day the morning talk show host, Mailman, popped his head into the office where I was busy pretending to enjoy organizing CDs aspiring artists would drop off in hopes of getting airtime. There were so many of them and they mostly ended up in File 13, aka the trash can.

I heard, "Hey, Maranda, come here for a second. I want you to do something for me." I stepped into the hallway as he went on to explain that they rarely have new voices in the building and that he needed me to be the voice on a commercial he was producing. I nervously wondered if I was the one for the job, but either way, I was happy to get a break from my usual monotonous office tasks.

Stepping into the room with the microphone, he instructed me to read the copy in a voice as if I were a stripper. There was a pause. I didn't say anything aloud, but in my mind, I responded with, "Excuse me?!"

He went on to say, "Just pretend like you're whispering into your boyfriend's ear." He gave me those instructions as he backed out of the room, letting me know that he would be outside waiting for me to finish.

There I was in a small dimly lit room, all alone with my imaginary boyfriend, also known as a microphone. I read the copy, whispered into the mic, and voilà. Just like that, I was a stripper from Detroit, or Atlanta, or Vegas coming to Mississippi to do the things that strippers do. My voice had officially been pimped out.

Apparently, my voice had a promising career as a stripper, because it wasn't long until Mailman invited me to hang out with him on the air during his morning show. "Just come in after you finish working around the office. We can call you The Intern."

It was the tipping point that gave me everything I needed to help me find my purpose. I had been completely undone when I found out that I had to stay in school another semester, but little did I know that fate would place me exactly where I needed to be.

It didn't take long for Stan Branson, the Program Director, to hear me on the air and eventually offer me a part-time job when a weekend jock quit on him. Of course, I took the job, which years later led to me being offered a full-time position as Maranda J on the same morning show that once knew me as The Intern. How many people can say that the first time they heard their voice on the radio was when they were pretending to be a stripper? My mom must've been so proud. Lucky for me, my one-night stand with the mic as a stripper didn't set the tone for my entire professional career. It did, however, prove how seemingly undesirable situations are only temporary and sometimes a necessary part of your journey.

Maybe that's where you are right now, and the reason you're reading this book. Maybe you are stuck at a job you hate, wishing you could be your own boss. Or maybe you are in a position at work that seems far removed from the position you deserve.

Here's the good news: how your career and journey begin doesn't determine where they end.

In my case, I started by spending an extra semester in college while going eight thousand dollars deeper in debt, in addition to pretending to be a stripper on the radio. No, it didn't mean I was destined for a life on the poles. These early experiences have become just a small piece of the story that helped me slide into a job at the radio station, which eventually led me to something even greater – finding my purpose.

For nearly fifteen years, I worked as an on-air radio personality at 99JAMS WJMI in Jackson, MS and it was during this time that I gained the confidence and insight I needed to one day quit my job and take a chance on myself as an entrepreneur.

I'm sure you've heard the phrase "trust the process." There is always a bigger picture. Most of the time we want to have all of the answers and to hear "yes" every time we ask for something. The sooner you get comfortable going with the flow as you move into the unknown, the sooner you will see growth.

Oftentimes when we are told no (like when I was told I couldn't graduate without that last class), we use it as an excuse to shut down or question whether we are on the right path. Hearing "no" or receiving rejection is simply the universe telling you to try something different. In turn, failure can also be the world's way of telling you to find another way. The next time you feel rejected, see it as a navigation system suggesting that you take another route.

On September 22, 2018, I took a chance on myself, quit my job, and began working toward what I felt was my true purpose: becoming an entrepreneur and full-time brand strategist. However, it wasn't until I started taking clients that I was able to see the connection between past experiences and life's purpose.

It seems we spend more time searching for purpose than we do living it. We spin our wheels searching for a deeper meaning in our current situations, when the truth is that the signs are always there, directing us to our purpose. To find them, all you have to do is turn around and look into your past. The signs directing you to your purpose have been there all along. Looking at my own life's patterns, I realize that I have always been drawn to people. I have always asked questions, searched for answers about why we do things, and been curious about the behavior of others.

This book is about what I've discovered on my journey to help entrepreneurs identify their authentic purpose, and then use that discovery to build a brand. I'm about to show you how you can do the same. If you are tired of playing it safe, turn the page, and in the words of Blackstreet, let's go back – way back into time. *Cue "Don't Leave Me" by Blackstreet.*

When your purpose is clearly defined and you can identify how you connect to your audience emotionally, it sets the tone for a more impactful brand.

1
FINDING PURPOSE IN YOUR PAST

In The Beginning There Was Branding

Have you ever wondered why learning history is such an important part of living in a society? When we look to the past it can help us understand behaviors and patterns. It can even tell us which direction to take in our current circumstances. More often than not, life – and history – seems to repeat itself. This was never more apparent to me than when I began meeting with clients as a brand strategist.

During my first few sessions, I realized I was helping people with more than just their branding. Unintentionally, I kept identifying and connecting people's past experiences in life to their current entrepreneurial ventures.

Over and over again I asked probing questions and listened intently to my clients' responses and their stories. At times during these sessions, the journey into the past would bring them to tears, but it also always brought clarity. As we uncovered these deeper emotions, I watched them sit in awe wondering how I made the connection from their childhood experiences to who they had become now.

I quickly realized that most of us are spending our lives trying to either give others something we were lacking as a child or attempting to share something we had in abundance.

What do we call this connection from our past to our present? More importantly, what do we do with it? It's called purpose, and we should use it to tell our truth.

It suddenly dawned on me that I wasn't just helping these people with their brand, I was identifying the purpose, or the why, in their lives and helping it make sense to them. I was giving them the invaluable gift of clarity, something most people spend their entire lives searching for. Together we were discovering the root of why they do what they do.

It was mind-blowing to finally feel like I was fulfilling my own purpose. And it was enchanting to discover that it was wrapped up in helping others find their own.

What is Purpose?

The dictionary app on my phone defines purpose as: "the reason for which something is done or created or for which something exists."

And there it is, clear as day.

If purpose is found in the root of why a thing exists, then why are so many of us looking for it in our current situations or our futures? Sure, we may see signs directing us in the present but why that's the right direction for us is always found in our past.

Let's take a look at one of my client's stories to better understand how this works. For the sake of this book, we will call her Nicole.

She is a former educator-turned-realtor. She came to me for help in making the jump into entrepreneurship with her first brokerage company. Like many entrepreneurs, she was a little uneasy but ready to make a change. She seemed to be a good real estate agent and was clearly a good educator I could tell by the way she color-coordinated and organized items on the dry erase board during our sessions. However, she was having a difficult time finding a way to make her new brokerage company stand out. During our first session, we didn't discuss her business, social media plans, or marketing strategies. We just talked about Nicole the person.

My clients are often surprised to discover that the first session is all about them, the person behind the business, not the actual business. They either show up nervous not knowing what to expect or they come with a pen and pad, ready to take a crapload of notes. Oftentimes, after this initial session, they realize that this was the therapy session they didn't know they needed.

This personal first session with my clients is essential in order to identify personal patterns and connect it to their brand message. Knowing and understanding your personal challenges, barriers, or self-sabotaging ways is vital to the growth of your businesses, especially as an entrepreneur. We all have challenges that have the potential to stand in the way of our success. If you can sit down and be honest with yourself long enough to identify them, then you can create a plan to manage your personal obstacles as you grow.

I asked Nicole to tell me about her oldest childhood memory. "What's the furthest back you can remember? Take me to that moment." You can imagine the look on an introvert's face when you ask them to tell you about a part of their life that they don't normally share with others. I had already given her the *trust the process* speech before diving into the questions, so she thought for a second and shared with me a memory that may not have been the first, but one that she could most vividly recall.

She told me about a time growing up when her father received a promotion at work, but there was a catch: the family had to relocate to Atlanta. Her father moved ahead of the rest of the family, to get their new home ready for her, her mother, and her sister.

As it turned out, it didn't go as planned. She didn't know what or why, but something went wrong. Her father returned home and their move to Atlanta was canceled.

Not only that but whatever happened required the family to downsize from a house to an apartment. Like most children, she and her sister adjusted but she remembered feeling like her life had changed forever. One day shortly after moving into the apartment, Nicole and her sister were lying in bed, joking around. Amidst the laughter, she turned to her sister and said, "I think we are poor." They continued laughing in their innocence.

At the end of her memory, as she said, "I guess I just feel like having a home is the foundation to a good family, no matter what the family looks like."

The moment gave me chills – I knew we had landed on something important. She had unconsciously created this belief as a child that living in an apartment was the reason her family dynamic had shifted. *And just like that, we had discovered her brand message.*

Often during sessions, once the nerves wear off, my clients will ease into opening up and it's in those moments when I usually find their purpose. Not only had we found a foundational message to build her brand upon, but we also had a unique and personal idea that would connect her to her buyers. Nicole believed that the foundation for a healthy family started with home ownership. This personal message connected Nicole to her consumers on an emotional level, making it authentic and impactful.

When your purpose is clearly defined and you can identify how you connect to your audience emotionally, it sets the tone for a more impactful brand.

When I started this work, I never imagined I would be giving people the thing I was lacking: A clear understanding of purpose.

Why Purpose is Important to You (the Entrepreneur)

On November 16, 2018, I launched my website asking the world to now refer to me as a brand strategist. Hopeful and scared, I put my brand out into the void, fingers crossed and praying people would show up. And they really did show up. I remember setting a goal of at least four clients a month. I had no idea that I would attract more than two hundred entrepreneurs in less than two years. My mind was blown.

During client sessions, I realized most entrepreneurs have the same recurring problems when it comes to their brand. It is often one of three things:
  ▸ Their message isn't clean and organized.

- They don't fully understand who they are talking to.
- They don't know how to show up on social media.

Can you see how these things all rely on each other? They all matter.

What was fascinating to me was the more I met with clients, the more I understood the power of including your purpose in your branding message. Not only was it evident how much the purpose matters to a business' audience, but I had the chance to witness over and over again how it affected the actual entrepreneur to find and make that connection for themselves. They would light up as if I had turned on a light bulb in their hearts. It was as if I had lit a fire under their asses, given them a kick in the pants, or introduced them to the love of their life.

Okay, I think you get the picture. They were shook.

This unexpected personal and professional connection to purpose and passion is priceless. Most of my clients responded with gratitude as they sat in shock expressing how they had never made those connections before, or how they had never shared their stories with anyone. I was – and am – still honored to be able to help so many talented entrepreneurs and to hear their stories. We all are deeply connected to our manifested dreams, and my clients are no different. They were all channeling their childhood desires through their businesses, and through my process they were finally able to see and know their purpose.

Okay, so now what? What do you do with purpose once you identify it? Do you add it to the mission statement and just stick it on your website?

No. You take that feeling and breathe it into your business. It is your brand. It is the thing you market even more than the thing you do. It is how you connect to your target audience on a deeper and more emotional level.

Branding is about how you make people feel through your products or services. Branding, done correctly, can bring success to your life and your business through purpose.

In a world where we are so disconnected, most of us want to feel seen. The moment a consumer finds a connection within a brand is the moment they are sold.

If there is a story they can personally relate to, they are more than sold, they have become a fan of your brand. When you connect to a fan's heart you simultaneously connect to their wallet.

Now let's go back to Nicole who enjoyed her job, but she felt something was missing. Not only did she need her clients to see her, but she needed them to feel seen. Identifying her unique brand voice was the secret sauce that connected her to her audience, and finding her genuine purpose in her work confirmed that she was on the right path.

The marketing may convince them to buy but it is the brand that makes them stay loyal for the long haul.

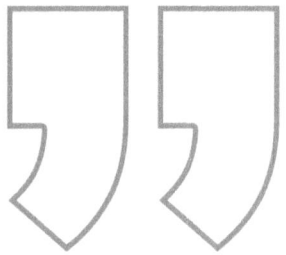

2
YOUR TARGET AUDIENCE HAS A NAME

Now that we understand purpose and how it connects to you and the person you serve the next step is to get to know your audience better. So many times, I hear entrepreneurs talking about how their product or service is for everybody. And while this may be the case for a few isolated products, the truth is that nothing is for everyone.

I find the getting to know your consumer part of the branding process is often challenging for my clients.

They worry that creating a single avatar for their brand is going to somehow isolate them from the rest of their audience. This could not be further from the truth. Creating a single avatar or ideal person for your brand helps you, the marketer, get specific in the way you speak to your audience.

(Stay with me here because this is so powerful. I know I said earlier that purpose was powerful but, this is too. Stay focused, you.)

Have you ever been scrolling through social media and come across a post that seemed like it was speaking directly to you? You know, like one of those posts where it felt like someone had hacked your texts, your brain, and your phone calls? The words come jumping off the screen and smack you in the face. Then before you know it, there you are, lying in bed at 2 A.M. on the checkout screen purchasing some super ninja vegetable cutters that you now believe you can't possibly live without. I will not confirm or deny that I've done this.

This is not a coincidence. These marketers know exactly who you are, down to your fears and behaviors. They have done the research and observed enough consumers to track habits and desires. And because they know you most intimately, they also know exactly what to say to grab your attention. They have designed a message targeted towards you, the single avatar. Doing this as an entrepreneur is a gamechanger. It helps you train your brain to speak to and meet a specific need for a specific buyer.

When you become clear in your communication about what needs you meet for the consumer, everyone with that unique need (no matter their profile) will want what you are selling.

When You Try to Talk to Everyone, You Don't Say Much of Anything

Have you ever attempted to go live on Instagram when suddenly your brain was overwhelmed by the thought of who would be watching and listening? Anxiety kicks in and while shaking, you hit the live button and start rambling. Then you try to speak to all the needs of every imaginary person that you think is tuning in. Meanwhile, people on the other side of the phone are starting to tune you out because you are taking too long to get to the point or you never make it clear why they should keep listening.

This is because you are not speaking with clarity to your

avatar or ideal client. What if instead of talking to everyone, you imagined that every time you go live you are Face Timing your one ideal target person to give them the information they need? Or if on every caption you wrote on your posts you were envisioning that you are really texting your ideal client and solving their problem. You would use pronouns like you and your instead of "hey guys" or "hey everyone."

When I first launched my business, I woke up every morning helping Bridget. She is a 33-year-old black woman. She is a nurse who wants to turn her side hustle into a business but isn't sure how. She doesn't have any kids and spends her free time traveling and hanging out with friends. She shops at Belk and Dillard's and is scared to leave this earth without finding and fulfilling her purpose. The most important thing to her is financial stability.

Bridget was – and is – my ideal target person. The moment I decided to wake up and only speak to her on social media was the day my business took off. Whenever I stop talking to her, my sales slowdown.

A strong niche and well-defined brand will hook the targeted audience every time. The marketing may convince them to buy but it is the brand that makes them stay loyal for the long haul.

How do you make your loyal consumers feel? This is when focusing on the 80/20 rule comes into play.

What is the 80/20 Rule?

You may have heard of this phrase when it comes to relationships. The 80/20 rule centers around the idea that one person can only meet eighty percent of your needs and the rest is up to you. In this case, it's the opposite. It's the twenty percent that is giving your business life and you should pay attention to them at all times.

Let me explain. Typically, about twenty percent of your audience is your loyal fanbase who will reliably follow you and your brand. These are the consumers who are emotionally invested in you. They will sustain you when you are experiencing low sales or engagement. These are the kind of consumers that will sing your praises on their social media or to their friends and family. Word of mouth referrals is the best form of advertisement.

Then there is the eighty percent. They are the ones that only come to you when you are running a sale and are usually on the fence about if they want to do business with you. They often come requesting changes in how you operate, or show up as a business with no intention of sticking around.

If you were to spend your time chasing the fair-weather eighty percent group, you risk neglecting your loyal audience. The goal is to invest in the twenty percent so that this share will increase as your awareness grows. Don't neglect your twenty percent. Instead, get to know them better and show up for them.

Understanding your target customer is key because if you don't know who you are talking to on a basic level, then you won't know how to serve them. And if you aren't serving others, why are you in business? Learn to speak their language in every aspect of your marketing.

I'm always instantly drawn to people that are like me. We all are. Nelson Mandela said, "If you talk to a man in a language he understands, that goes to his head. If you talk to him in his own language, that goes to his heart."

While Mandela wasn't speaking about branding and marketing, it undoubtedly applies here as well. Remember, the ultimate goal in selling is an *emotional connection*. When you connect to someone's heartstrings, you are also connecting to their wallet. Most purchases are emotional and based on how something makes the customer feel. Keep that in mind the next time you are talking to your ideal target person. How you make them feel matters and impacts your bottom line.

Let's Not Make This All About You

It is easy to think "If you build it, they will come." People will indeed find you with a clearly defined brand and the right marketing strategy.

But what will sustain you is being sure that what you do is centered around serving others in some capacity.

It's true that if it appeals to you, it'll certainly appeal to others; but if it is all about you and your ego then your growth is limited. This type of mindset happens more often than not in business. It shows up when entrepreneurs talk about how privileged you should feel to work with them or when they lash out at customers for asking recurring questions or for getting on their nerves.

Of course, it's a privilege to work with you, you're a downright badass because you are out here taking a chance on yourself and your ability to generate money with your skillset. But when the dust settles the consumer should be the one left feeling like a badass for working with you. They should never feel beneath you. It's a thin line but I think you get the picture.

We live in a world where people feel more alone than connected through social media. Anxiety, stress, and depression are the most prevalent mental illnesses in the United States. Many people join fraternities, sororities or groups to feel like they are a part of something bigger than themselves.

At the root of most behavior is a desire to be seen, so be the type of business that sees people. Then prove to them that you are worth the connection. The best way to know what your audience loves about you is to give yourself permission to be who you are.

One brand I can think of that does this well is Chick-fil-A. They have built a sense of warmth and kindness around chicken of all things. I'm going to break down exactly how they achieve this later on but for now, just know that they're an excellent example of how a company has mastered emotional connection.

Take some time to discover your target audience, and how your brand answers the needs of your consumers.

The better you can comprehend your target audience, or your ideal target person, the more accurately you will be able to build your business around them. Remember, nothing is set in stone so be flexible, stay fluid, and learn to pivot when it's needed.

Now, let's get connected.

The truth is that it's not healthy or safe to play it small.

3
DREAM BIG

When did we stop dreaming? My mother wrote a few children's books when I was younger. One was created from a poem she had written, and another was a chapter book featuring my late sister and me as characters. I can remember lying in bed in 1992 listening to her read these stories. The characters were as much a part of my upbringing as Saturday morning cartoons and cereal.

I can't help but wonder why after all those years my mother never published her books. I'm pretty sure she suffered from what we now know as imposter syndrome.

It seems like at some point when we shift into adulthood we stop dreaming. We limit our imagination and start focusing on short term goals that somehow feel safer to our adult brains. The truth is that it's not healthy or safe to play it small. This type of mindset is rooted in fear. It's a false sense of control that doesn't actually protect us.

Four Things to Help You Dream Big

Let's talk about your mindset. Keep in mind (no pun intended) that your mindset is a constant work for the entirety of your career. Hell, it's constant work for the rest of your life. Mindset by definition is the established set of attitudes held by someone, so I'm sure you can see how paying attention to your behaviors and patterns can help you stay on track.

Here are a few things that you can practice to help you maintain a successful mindset:

1. Accept that fear will always be a part of your life and then make a plan to mitigate it. The antidote to fear is action. Feel the fear and do it anyway.

2. Accept the fact that you are not for everyone. This will help you to focus on the people that are for you.

3. Create a routine. Listen to podcasts. Dance every day. Meditate. Practice intentional thinking. Create a routine that works with your schedule and repeat it as often as possible.

4. Write your vision and dreams down multiple times a week. I can't express enough how much power there is in writing things out on paper. Typing messages with your thumbs may save you time, but writing things out will change your life.

What next? It's time to ignite your imagination and dream big about the type of business you desire to have. I was surprised to discover how many entrepreneurs never took the time to imagine their business in its most successful state. If we never put a destination in our mental GPS then how will we know how to prepare for the trip?

Make time every week to dream big. If we don't know where we are going then we can't properly plan for the ride.

A lot of you fell into entrepreneurship out of necessity or because you did something well and someone convinced you to start a business. But problems can pop up when you rush past the vision and planning phase.

Take some time this week to sit still and imagine in the most detailed way what you want your business to look like in its most successful state. Imagine all the big, beautiful, successful things that scare you. That's when you know you're doing it right.

Then come back here and start packing everything you need for your trip to reach your dream destination.

It's understandable if you are struggling a little to go there because we have been conditioned to think small. So, here is a little help on what to ask yourself:

- If you were given ten million dollars to start a business, what would it look like?

- If you could be famously known for anything in the world, what would it be?

- If you were already rich and could do anything with your time for free, what would it be?

Now imagine all of the possibilities your heart desires. Imagine them with no obstacles in front of you or your business.

Commit yourself to practice seeing the bigger picture for the rest of your life. Your future you will thank you for it.

Clarity and speed are your best friends.

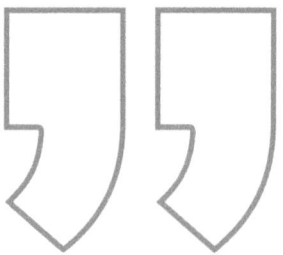

4
THE ELEVATOR PITCH

In the Middle There Was Organization

It's a good rule of thumb to pretend that everyone listening to you talk about your business is thinking to themselves: "Get to the point." I know it is easy to believe that people want to hear all of the details which you hold dear to your heart when it comes to your business. But the truth is that most people are self-serving. Including you.

Sometimes when we are nervous, we ramble on from one random thought to another. We start connecting our thoughts together with an occasional "and um," until it all starts to sound like one big sea of words and a never-ending story. Eventually, we end up leaving the person listening in a daze trying to fish out the point. Does this sound familiar? Whether it's you or someone you know, we can all relate to this.

There are two types of people when it comes to networking: the one drowning someone with their words or the one trying to not drown in the sea of someone else's endless thoughts. If I am being honest, I have been on both sides of the spectrum. You don't have to own up to which one you are to benefit from this chapter, just know it's dedicated to helping you form your elevator pitch.

Pitch What?

Let's be clear about one thing: tossing your credentials out to a person that you are meeting for the first time will never be natural. For most of us, it feels a bit boastful, and in some cases, we can even end up sounding pretentious. But what if we flipped the way that we positioned ourselves when we pitched? What if we focused on the value provided more than we focused on ourselves? This can be a gamechanger when it comes to how you network.

The trick here is to spend less time in your pitch talking about yourself and more time explaining the impact you make as a result of what you do.

When you are quickly able to tell people who you are and what emotional need you meet for others, they will in turn quickly be able to understand where to put you in their lives. And isn't this the ultimate goal? Clarity and speed are your best friends.

Elevator Pitch Tips

The first tip in pitching is *knowing who you are pitching to*. This is so important when you are thinking about how to frame your pitch. Knowing what they care the most about will help you determine what to lead with. You can't understand how they think if you haven't identified who they are.

A few years back I was in a room full of women at a conference in Atlanta. They were all entrepreneurs; the moderators were allowing the crowd to pass the mic and ask questions. I noticed that everyone who grabbed the mic would give a quick introduction of themselves then ask their question. At the time I didn't have a question, but I couldn't pass up the opportunity to let people in this room know what value I could provide. So, I quickly thought of a question centered around team building because at the time I was in search of an assistant. I raised my hand and when the mic came to me, I said,

"Hello, my name is Maranda Joiner and I am a brand strategist. I help entrepreneurs identify their purpose and weave that into their brand messaging, so they know what to say on social media to make money." Then I proceeded to ask my question.

When the panel was over, and everyone was moving on to the next session, I stood still in the exact place that I was when I asked my question. And wouldn't you know it, several people bee lined to me to give me business cards and inquire about my services. I booked two new clients and even found my first virtual assistant in that room. Being intentional and concise will get you booked.

This brings me to the second tip. *Be intentional.* What is your goal? What are you hoping to accomplish with this pitch? Is it networking? Landing a sale? Funding? Before you open your mouth to introduce yourself to a room, you should know what your intentions are. Intentions produce results and being clear about them before you speak will keep you from talking about things that don't matter.

Tip number three is to *write your pitch down and practice*. Practice in the mirror and practice with a smile on your face. Smiling helps you to come across as approachable in person and it helps you to connect over the phone. Remember to pause and either let the other person speak when it's one-on-one or pause for feedback if it's a presentation. Avoid long stories that require you to connect a lot of dots and get to the point as quickly as possible. Don't forget to be inclusive of your audience.

The final tip is to *make sure you close the deal*. Be clear about what actionable steps you want to take. What do you want the end result to be? I can't tell you how many DMs I receive on social media where people introduce themselves and end the message with "We should connect and work together." I don't know what to do with that. Work together how? It should not be left up to the person you are trying to connect with to figure that out. Know what you want and be clear and detailed about it. If you don't know what you want, then you aren't ready to pitch. If you find yourself not knowing what you want, then refer back to the second tip: be intentional.

A good framework for your pitch is to answer these few questions.

- Who are you?
- Who do you serve?
- What problem do you solve?
- What is your unique position?
- What is your ask?

When you master answering these questions you are well on your way to forming the perfect pitch. Don't get too attached to your answers though because every once in a while, you will need to be flexible enough to alter it as the situation calls for it.

Story Matters at the Right Time

I believe everyone has a story worth sharing but at the same time, I know there is a time and place for everything. When we first meet someone, especially in a networking setting, we have to assume they are not instantly interested in who we are in so much depth. What is special to us isn't always special to the people we encounter. Therefore, with each engagement, we should imagine that we only have a small window to catch their attention and emotionally hook them before we lose them.

Most of us make the mistake of assuming that everyone is as excited about our business as we are. That's just not the case. It's our job to explain clearly and concisely why they should care.

Start with the part of your story that matters to them, not the part that matters to you. And when they show more interest in something you say, this is when you say more about that area. If they don't show interest, you move on to the next point.

A key part of networking effectively is being able to read social cues. Did they ask a follow-up question? Did their face show interest or did they change subjects? These are indicators that they may or may not be interested in what you do. And either way, that's okay. You aren't for everyone. No one is.

It all goes back to branding. What emotional fulfillment are they getting? Make your answer simple and get to the point when you are answering these three questions: who you are, what you do for others, and why they should care.

If you can't articulate what your business is about then how can anyone else understand what you are about?

The most important thing is to ensure that your words can easily become actions.

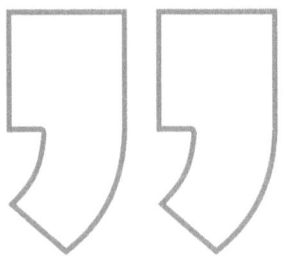

5
A MISSION STATEMENT YOU CAN FEEL

Branding is about how you make people feel. I can't say this enough. Once you identify this feeling, it then becomes your job to breathe that feeling into the consumer experience. Believe it or not a lot of entrepreneurs start their businesses with little to no strategy. And sometimes even the vision is blurry. I am amazed to discover how many people are operating without a clear vision other than making money. This is a dangerous space to be in because if you aren't clear about the destination then you are more likely to head in every direction. This results in feeling like you are all over the place.

Sound familiar? You can put a plan in place and still be open to a detour, but you have to put a clear destination in the GPS so you can know how to pack for the trip. And like most trips, something is bound to go wrong. But just like any good traveler, you are built to figure it out. The beautiful thing about being your own boss is that you have the freedom to be flexible. Matter of fact, it's necessary for your survival.

Mission Statement

Your mission statement does not have to be perfect but it does have to be something that you can easily put into action. One of my favorites examples of a brand that is living out its mission in real life is Chick-fil-A. For those of you that may not be familiar, Chick-fil-A is a fast-food restaurant that serves chicken. Chicken nuggets, chicken sandwiches, chicken soup, chicken salad, chicken wraps – I think you get the picture. Talk about niching down.

Their mission statement is "to glorify God by being a faithful steward of all that is entrusted to us. To have a positive influence on all who come in contact with

Chick-fil-A." I always picture in my head that the owners started their business and built it around a feeling. I imagine that they identified the way they wanted to make people feel and then they chose a fast-food restaurant as the way to deliver that feeling. They sell chicken with pleasure by drilling it into their employee's heads to say "my pleasure" over and over again. They go above and beyond to bring their mission to life consistently by allowing you to order a million sauces without questioning your request. I don't have to explain to them that my son likes to mix sriracha and Polynesian sauce together; or that I prefer BBQ sauce with my fries. No matter how many sauces I ask for, it's always "my pleasure."

I can recall a time I pulled up to the drive-thru, ordered my food, and was about to pay when I realized I had left my wallet across the street at work. I asked the lady at the window if she would hold my order while I ran back to get my card. To my surprise, she looked me square in my eyes and with a smile on her face said, "Don't worry about it! We'll just ring it up the next time you eat with us," as she handed me my order. I was shocked, and my stomach was grateful because your girl was starving and pressed for time. I couldn't believe that she trusted me to return with the money. And now that I think about it, I don't think I ever went back to pay. But, I'm not on trial here.

My point is that this is how you take your mission and breathe it into your business. Your mission statement should be something that you can put into action. It's not meant to be full of jargon that most of the people you serve never use. The mission sets the tone for your business and determines the journey of your customers or clients. Don't overcomplicate it. Start with the feeling and then plan out in detail exactly how you want to deliver that feeling. The most important thing is to ensure that your words can easily become actions.

Vision Statement

The vision statement is not the same as your mission statement. The mission statement is the work you do, but the vision, well that is what you are hoping to see in this world as a result of the work you do. It's the big picture – the dream. This is the moment you drop from your head to your heart and remember why you even started your business in the first place. Your vision should come from a place of service and heart, and not from a place of execution.

I often use Dr. Martin Luther King Jr. as an example of

this. Years after he was murdered, the world is still displaying his vision through murals and quotes, reminding us all of his hopes and dreams. He hoped to see the day when his children would be judged by the content of their character and not by the color of their skin. He dreamt of black people being free at last and of seeing people of different races coming together in unity.

Now his mission on the other hand – the way he worked – was different. His mission carried him into dangerous situations. He often traveled into places of racial darkness to shed light on injustices by rallying African American leaders to support his vision. Many times, his mere presence challenged racial segregation and racists. His mission was the work that needed to be done to fulfill his vision. This is how you take your mission and use it to fuel the bigger picture which is your vision.

Core Values

There's one more thing we need you to identify – core values. These beliefs serve as a continuation to support your mission and vision. They are the principles that guide the actions of your company. They are the cornerstones on which your business is built. For example, some of Chick-fil-A's core values are *customer first, personal excellence, continuous improvement, working together, and stewardship.* Core values are the beliefs that hold everything together like glue. Core values set the tone not just for how you show up, but for how the pieces of your business work together. It determines the culture of your business. Don't make the mistake of focusing so much on making money that you find yourself grinding away and chasing it without a mission, clear vision, or core values. Speaking of money...

If you aren't consistent in your rates and structure, then you don't have a business, you have a hobby.

6
GET OUT YOUR FEELINGS

This whole book is centered around relationships, and in this section, we're delving into one of the toughest: our relationship with money. There are so many factors to consider as an entrepreneur when setting a price.

One of the first things I recommend is facing your own insecurities about money. Sit down and have an honest look at your relationship with it. I often tell my son that money is energy and before we can make it, we have to let go of the fear of not having it. Those of us who have attached an unhealthy fear of it will have trouble making it work for us. Money is energy and when you learn how to manage and generate the type of energy to bring it to you, you will never be broke a day in your life.

I can't think of many entrepreneurs that haven't struggled with determining prices. It's difficult to find that sweet spot between selling yourself short and scaring people off with a too high price. It can be overwhelming and difficult to make the right decision. One thing to keep in mind is that what may work for someone else's business may not work for yours. In addition to setting a fair price, we have to have an honest conversation about the service we provide living up to the prices we set.

I used to host events called A Lot Alike where entrepreneurs could come and mingle with other entrepreneurs that were just like them in their pursuit of success. The room would be full of seasoned experts, and new entrepreneurs. We would have open discussions about the ups and downs of entrepreneurship and some of the pain points that we experienced in business. It became evident the more we talked that we all are a lot more alike than we are different.

Finance was always a consistent topic. My friend, a multifaceted entrepreneur, was a guest at one of these events, and he said something that stuck with me. He stated that a lot of times we make the mistake of setting prices based on our self-worth when we should be setting prices based on the value we bring with the work that we do. There is a difference.

There are so many factors to consider; I'll share a few with you to get you headed in the right direction.

One of the first things you want to consider when setting your pricing is calculating what each transaction costs you. Add up the costs that go into making the product or providing that service. This includes the actual materials or labor that go into providing that service, as well as the rent you pay for your office or the equipment you use. These are direct and indirect costs.

Next, you want to look at your market and see what your competitors are charging for similar services. This gives you an idea of what your audience is willing to pay.

And finally, you want to consider your consumer. Understanding who they are and what they are willing to pay for your products and services is critical to the success of your business. Don't be afraid to test your audience, ask questions and make adjustments when you can.

Once you find your sweet spot, stay consistent long enough for your audience to adjust. Don't make the mistake of changing your price every month trying to cater to every pushback or complaint you receive about pricing. Do your research and put your stake in the ground about your pricing.

Because the truth is that if you aren't consistent in your rates and structure, then you don't have a business, you have a hobby.

How Does Your Brand Make You Feel?

One day I was in Sam's Club when my phone rang. I answered it and on the other line was my graphic designer. The frustration in his voice was apparent as he was venting to me about his client that had no clue how they wanted their brand to look, yet they were expecting him to bring it to life visually. They had given him minimal input about their business outside of the basic facts: name, slogan colors, and service. Well, wouldn't you know it, when he sent over a few logo options the client was frustrated because it "wasn't what they had in mind."

But then the question was left to ask, how would a graphic designer know what's on your mind unless you provided adjectives to help them bring it to life? The short answer is that they wouldn't know because they are not psychic – they are, however, creatives.

He concluded that his clients needed to see someone like me (a brand strategist) before they came to him. Someone to walk them through understanding their unique brand voice as well as understanding their audience. He concluded that they need someone to help them understand what their brand feels like beyond the words and titles.

What adjectives would you use to describe your business if it were a person? Would they be fun? Funny? Organized and punctual? If your business were a vacation destination, where would it be and what are the things about that place that feel like your business? Is it Bali or Mexico? Does it feel like Austin, Texas, or maybe Disneyland? When you start thinking about your business in this way you are now ready to list out words to help a graphic designer visually bring your brand to life. You can't just walk up and deposit money into them like a vending machine with little to no input and get a desired snack. Even with vending machines, you have to give clear input. As a brand strategist, I work with clients to help them figure these things out.

So, before you reach out to a graphic designer, do the above exercise. Use as many adjectives that come to mind, write them down and send them over to your graphic designer along with all of your other information. Not only will they be thankful that you did the work, but they will hopefully be closer to building the brand that you are envisioning in your heart.

A LOT ALIKE

Social media can be such a vulnerable space and sometimes it can feel like you're standing in front of someone naked asking them to love you.

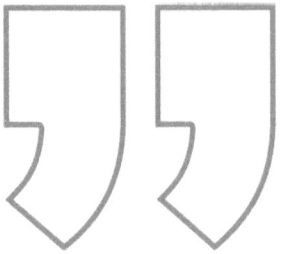

7
HOW TO COURT AND DATE YOUR AUDIENCE

Marketing is Just the Beginning

I was born in the 1980s, and I know what dating was like before there were cell phones and texting. I remember late night conversations on the house phone, and getting to know someone by asking questions, talking, and sharing laughter until the sun came up. This was the original engagement before people started using overly edited pictures and videos to tell a story that may or may not be the truth about who they are. This is what I think is wrong with social media today. Somewhere along the way, we lost the authentic act of engagement, yet it is what we claim we desire the most. It is what these apps were created for.

How do you get engagement without actually engaging? You don't. One of the top complaints I hear from clients is how their audience isn't engaging enough with the content they post. Instead of complaining, you need to ask the hard questions first: Do you know your audience well enough to approach them and talk to them? Are you getting to know them by engaging with them first? And are you sharing and talking about stuff that they want to hear? Are you likable? There is a misunderstanding about what kind of engagement we should be focused on the most. We tend to throw the word engagement around so much that nobody is considering how we have completely changed the meaning of the word when it comes to what we should care about in business. We have the definition all messed up. Before the algorithm was born, businesses had to rely on real-life interactions and engagement to determine how well their business was doing. But somewhere along the way the number of followers on a social platform took over and started clouding the line of worth and value. Engagement doesn't have to be so complicated.

It's Time to Date Your Audience

What if when you showed up with your business or brand you decided to "date" your target audience instead of selling to them? In reality, this is what is happening. You are courting your audience.

Social media can be such a vulnerable space and sometimes it can feel like you're standing in front of someone naked asking them to love you.

I get it and believe me this is why it is so hard for most of us to do it. But let's all do a self-check here. How comfortable are you with vulnerability in other areas of your life? I struggle with this daily. It's understandable why most of us battle with showing up on social media.

We have to ask ourselves: What do we want this dating experience to be like? Setting the mood is everything and just like in the oh so-awkward-world of dating, you want your target audience to know who you are, like you as a business, and trust you enough to invest in you. Let's talk about how to make the first move.

What type of dater are you? Are you the awkward and shy one that doesn't say much of anything? Or are you the type to constantly talk about yourself, never pausing to let the person get a word in edgewise? You must work on finding the balance of being somewhere in the middle when it comes to your business.

Maybe you've got this mastered. You know exactly how to share just enough information about your business to keep the audience interested and encouraged. You make them laugh, you ask all of the right questions to get them talking, and then to seal the deal, you bring value to the conversation by sharing something helpful that they care about. Rinse and repeat.

If you maintain this rotation of posting, not only will your audience like you, but they will feel like they genuinely know you. And people engage with people they feel close to and more importantly, people spend money with those they trust. You should make it your first priority to create this type of vibe on your social media.

Branding is how you make people feel, marketing is how you convey your message. Simply put, it's the amplification of your message. Once we know whom we are speaking to and what we want to say, it's time to "date" our target person.

Categories make everything better. The mind naturally wants to put things in categories and so by doing this on social media, it helps you to not feel so overwhelmed about posting. There is a thing called the Rule of Thirds where you have three pillars that you post under. The Rule of Thirds simply states that one-third of the time you want to post statuses that promote who you are so people can know you. Another third of the time you want to post statuses that engage with your audience so they will like you. And finally, one-third of the time you want to share valuable information with your audience so they will trust you. Rinse and repeat. Let's take a closer look at each one.

Know You

The other day I heard a McDonald's commercial. It was an advertisement telling me that the McRib sandwich was coming back. Then I thought to myself, "Oh yeah, I forgot about that sandwich," and from that to, "Man I haven't had McDonald's in a long time, and a McRib sandwich sounds nice right about now." Now let me be clear, I am not a McDonald's fan. I hardly ever think about eating there. But I bet that even if you aren't a McDonald's fan either you at least imagined the sandwich in your mind just now. The McRib comes around at least once a year and they still run ads for it. More importantly, they constantly run commercials for other menu items that never go away.

I think it's safe to say that a company that has been around since the 1950s is pretty well known. So why would they still need to advertise when there is a McDonald's in proximity to almost every neighborhood? They advertise because if they didn't, you would forget about them. They advertise because when you go to bed at night your brain resets. So, you have to ask yourself the question, if decades later, McDonald's is still McDonalding, why am I worried that I promote my business too much? The short answer is that you shouldn't be worried.

Someone out there needs to be reminded about why they need you.

Someone out there needs to hear about you for the first time and someone out there needs to hear what you have to offer.

People won't know who you are if you don't tell them. As an entrepreneur, it is your job to paint the picture for your audience.

One-third of the time when you post, make it clear who you are and what you do. This can be a simple post stating facts about your brand, or this can look like a story about the work you do. Even testimonies from clients can reveal who you are. Being crystal clear about these things leaves little room for confusion.

People need to know where to put you in their life, and clarity helps you come to mind when that need arrives. Simple storytelling is all it takes.

Remember, you are painting a picture of who you are, one stroke at a time.

Like You
Have you ever been on a date with someone and all they did was talk about themselves? Or maybe you have a friend that does this and won't let you get a word in edgewise, but as soon as they are done, they are ready to end the conversation. Now think about how those engagements make you feel. Not so good, right? Well, this is how some of us show up in our business. We don't take the time to actually listen to our audience. Hell, we barely even talk to them sometimes. But how else do you expect to get to know them if you don't ask questions or most importantly, listen? This is where the real

engagement counts. Nobody wants to be connected to someone that only talks about the products and services they offer.

Asking the right questions to your audience is key in connecting to them. And doing things to make them like you can be a gamechanger. This is the part of the date where you are getting to know each other. These questions can be about anything – they don't have to always be about the business. If you sell cookware, maybe ask questions about their favorite go-to meals to make after a busy day, but also feel free to ask about their favorite movies too.

Engagement is about building a relationship, not numbers. You want your audience to know you aren't a robot. They are real human beings, and they desire emotional connection just like you. Take time to click on and like the posts, leave comments, and network. When you do this, your audience becomes interested in who you are, and in some cases, they start to feel like they know you. People naturally want to do business with people they know and like. Not only that but holding their attention on a post with a well thought out question can boost the algorithm and help you to be more visible on their timeline. So be likable.

Trust You

It's a given that people do business with people they trust, yet trust seems to be a tricky thing for people to gain. I think most people don't understand how to build it within a relationship when it comes to business. Of course, being a person of your word or delivering consistently on a service will build trust with your audience, but what about the audience that you haven't done business with? What about the audience that is still considering doing business with you? This is where positioning yourself as the expert comes into play.

Giving valuable or helpful information is a good way to seal the deal. And I know you're probably thinking, "The game is to be sold not told." But the truth of the matter is that there isn't anything you can tell me that I can't Google or look up on YouTube. So why not be the source for your audience? You want to be strategic in how much you share, but don't be stingy. Give tips and remind people why they need you and your service. Share information without asking for anything in return so that when you finally do ask, the spirit of reciprocity kicks in.

Let them know you are qualified to do what you do.

Trust builds connections that are positive, optimistic, and fruitful. The process can be tricky so here are a few tips that are essential when building a dependable trust with your target audience:

Make valuable connections

I believe that what we put out into this world comes back to us. In some circles they call it sowing and reaping. In other spaces they say, "you get what you give." Making valuable connections is a way to show that you are someone to be trusted. When your audience witnesses you connecting to others it validates your trustworthiness.

Address issues directly

Nothing is more off putting than when a business or a brand dances around an issue. In a perfect world we would never have to worry about problems arising in our businesses. But unfortunately, there will come a time in every business when a problem will require your full attention. Honesty and accountability are the best ways to approach issues you may have along the way and taking care of your consumers and relying on the truth will gain trust every time.

Be engaging

Trust is almost impossible to gain without actually spending time with someone or getting to know them on a deeper level. This is probably one of the most powerful ways to build connections. But here is the part that most entrepreneurs forget; getting to know someone is a two-way street. So, practice sharing pieces of you with your audience. This can be as simple as the type of beverage you prefer or your favorite time of year. Just remember to be consistent and share authentically.

Bonus points when you realize that these tips apply to your everyday relationships as well.

Now that we know how to set intentions for your social media posts, we can talk about how to show up on the various platforms. There are far too many to keep up with but let's address the big three and possibly an up and coming one. Let's take your engagement to a whole new level.

> If we could learn to stop observing the number count and start observing the behavior of our following, then we could better scale our businesses and grow our brands.

8
THE WIDE, WIDE WORLD OF SOCIAL MEDIA

Let's pause here because before we dive deep into the ocean that is social media. We first have to identify the main problems we all face when it comes to social media. During client sessions, I realized most entrepreneurs have the same recurring problems when it comes to their brand. It is often one of three things:

- Their message isn't clean and organized.
- They don't fully understand who they are talking to.
- They don't know how to show up on social media.

Can you see how these things all rely on each other? They all matter.

And this unfortunate shift in the way we view engagement robbed us of the ability to see these social apps as tools. It robbed us of the ability to show up as the thing we need to be – ourselves. These apps don't define our worth as a business; it's quite the opposite, they actually serve as tools to give us feedback on what our consumers like and dislike.

If we could learn to stop observing the number count and start observing the behavior of our following, then we could better scale our businesses and grow our brands. It's a data game, not a numbers game.

And here is the best part: when we learn how to read the data that these apps give us and pivot our business and brands to adjust, the numbers will come. Say it with me: social media is a tool I use to help me better understand what my audience likes and dislikes.

Back in the day when Marvin Gaye or Whitney Houston showed up to a venue to perform, I imagine that it didn't matter if there were fifty or fifty thousand people present, because when they showed up, they didn't shrink down to the size of the crowd. You should be the same way with your brand.

No matter if you receive twelve likes or twelve hundred, just keep showing up. Paying attention to the patterns and using that information to determine your next move is how you win.

Speaking of showing up, have you ever asked yourself why you are on social media in the first place? What is your intention for being on there? Now if you are this far along in the book, I hope you at least know these two things: one, how you or your business makes people feel and two, who that specific person is that needs to feel it. If you don't then pause and take a minute to think about it and then continue on.

More than half the world is engaged in some way on social media sites. Some are even addicted to it in some way shape or form. It seems to be an alternate reality or escape for many. According to Digital Marketing, people are on social media for an average of two hours and three minutes every day. I believe it is more than that but I'm not the expert here. The point is that in all likelihood, your target audience is somewhere on social media right now waiting on you to get a message to them. Yet here you are afraid to post or even worse, you are posting and then running to hide behind a bush waiting for people to "engage" so it can validate your posting.

When thinking about the different platforms, one of the first things to consider is *which one is your ideal audience on*? In some cases, you can discover this by identifying the one that gives you the most engagement. Everything diverts back to your target audience. Think about the person you are serving and where they are spending their time and look at demographics. Most people are using Facebook, Instagram, TikTok, and even Clubhouse to generate leads. Depending on your target, you may even do well on Linkedin. Test these platforms and watch the level of engagement you receive. Pick the two platforms with the most engagement and engage, engage, engage.

The second thing to consider is *the language of that platform*. That's right, I bet you didn't know that each platform has its own language. Let's break it down.

There are a huge variety of social media channels. Each one is different and therefore should be approached differently. But they all have a specific way they project information to their audience. They are designed to communicate in unique ways to cater to all types of communicators. Haven't you ever wondered why some people love some platforms over others? It's because we all process information differently.

Facebook

People flock to Facebook to talk. They want to have real conversations with people they know, whether from back in the day or with a family member. They love to chat with people in their Facebook groups, and even with strangers. They want to know what is happening in your business or with your products. Heck, they will watch an entire six-minute video about it. They want to talk and engage with the people behind the curtains. So, this is how you show up – ready to talk. You want to share the things that help them understand who you are: life cycles, events, brand awareness, and compelling conversations. They want to know your story.

Instagram

Those who are especially active on Instagram are visually driven. With them, you want to use visually appealing pictures and stories to communicate to them. This can be behind-the-scenes videos, pictures from a photoshoot, funny dance videos, or reels. Instagram will even tell you (if your page is set to business) when your followers are on social media, who they are and where they live. Using the features and data to your advantage will help you not only show up better in the algorithm, but it will help you show up in all the ways people like to engage on the platform.

Twitter

Twitter is an information platform. Thoughts are shared in a way to provide quick communication. People go to Twitter for news, sports, and information. Hell, some people even check Twitter before they check the news. Even a screenshot of a tweet posted on my Instagram page has higher engagement than other posts. It's my personal belief that because Twitter has a reputation for being a source of intellectual news and important breaking information that people equate tweets to facts.

Clubhouse

Clubhouse is also an up-and-coming social site that is still in beta form as I am writing this book; it already has over one million users and is valued at one billion dollars. I can't imagine how much it will have grown by the time you are reading this. As an early user, I can say that in a short time it has revolutionized the world of networking amongst entrepreneurs, creatives, and the industry as a whole. One of the developers, Paul Davison stated that he wanted to "scale intimacy" and I can't unhear it.

The best way to describe Clubhouse is like a conference in your hand without having to leave your couch or get dressed. It has eliminated the overload of pictures or videos, and taken back the basics of human connection and conversations. It's an invite-only community and is built focusing on the user experience. They are literally building the app around us as we experience it and give feedback. Then the developers apply the feedback in real-time. I have never seen anything like it. If you can't tell, it has become one of my favorite apps to date. The extrovert in me is doing cartwheels. Not to mention that it could not have come to light at a better time than amid a pandemic when so many people are starving for human connection.

Speaking of connection, I hope by now you have learned to look at these apps as a way to connect to and understand your audience, and not as a way to validate your worth as a business. Clubhouse is not only useful in networking at an accelerated speed but you also have the opportunity to be exposed to your audience and their pain points by hosting rooms or listening to their questions in other rooms. Once the information is processed, you can use the data and engagement to help you understand what works for your audience and make real-time adjustments just like the developers of Clubhouse. Use interactions on your statuses and complaints to improve your business, and not as a reason to quit. Find the flow of posting and a rhythm that works for you and your audience on social media and before you know it, you will be in a committed relationship with your ideal target person.

Captions

Zig Ziglar has a story about a woman that would cut the end off of her ham before she cooked it. I'm not sure if this story was about his wife or not but let's visit it as an example on how it pays to ask the right questions.

One evening a husband sat reading the newspaper as he watched his wife prepare a ham for dinner. He watched as she cut the end off of the ham before placing it in the pan. He saw this as a waste of good ham and so he asked, why do you always cut the end off of the ham every time you make it. She said, "That's the way my mom prepared the ham." He then asked, "Well, why did she cut the end off?" The wife didn't know. So, later on that night she called her mom to find out why she cut the end of the ham off and her mom said, "Well, because that's the way my mom prepared ham." So, she decided to reach out to her grandfather since her grandmother had passed some years back to find out if he knew why her granny cut the end of the ham off before cooking it. He paused for a moment and said, "So it would fit into the pan." It turned out they just didn't have a big enough pan to fit it and were either too cheap to purchase another one or didn't care to.

There is such a good lesson to learn here not only in communication but just simply in asking the right questions. The lady in the story wasted so much ham over the years because she never took the time to ask, "Why?" Why do other businesses advertise the way they do? Why did they choose those captions and colors? Why did they pick that particular font?

All this time the ham lady was showing up with a false and unclear narrative because she was copying her mom instead of doing what made sense for her life. So many times, in marketing we do this very same thing.

We look at how other businesses are showing up with their brand and we don't consider that what works for their brand doesn't necessarily work for our brand and audience. It's so important to do the research and test your audience.

Take the time to figure out what they like by observing what they respond to more than you pay attention to what the competition is doing.

Once you understand your audience better it will be easier for you to speak their language. This will assist you in writing more compelling captions.

Now that you know to stay in your own lane when it comes to messaging, let's talk captions. There are multiple ways to write a caption. You employ storytelling, or you can speak directly to your audience. But one of the most impactful ways is to identify the problem you solve for your target person and then show them how you are the solution. Then wrap it up with a call to action giving them clear direction on what to do next.

We tend to assume that people already know their problems or that they automatically know what they need. That's not always the case. Most of us are so used to adjusting and adapting that we don't realize that there is a better way to operate. And in some cases, we have been doing a thing one way so long that it no longer seems like a problem. In turn, we are stuck in patterns that don't serve us. When writing out captions for social media you have the opportunity to bring that problem to the forefront. With social media, you can bring your message to life using visuals and words.

It is important to understand your ideal person and to identify their needs so you can serve them. By definition as an entrepreneur, it is your job to solve a problem or fulfill a desire. You can't bully them into spending money, instead you have to woo them.

Consistency is Key

When entrepreneurs are told to be consistent, for some reason they translate that to frequency. These two words are not the same, but when people hear consistency, they automatically think they have to show up and post three times a day, every day. And somewhere along the way we have set unrealistic expectations for what consistency looks like in real life.

Consistency on one hand can look like showing up on the same day at the same time. Whether that is three times a week or once a week. The goal is to figure out what works for your audience and then consistently give them that. Frequency on the other hand is the rate at which something occurs. You can decide the frequency you want to post, plan it out and then show up consistently. These two words used together can help you grow your audience.

A good practice is to choose a day to plan out all of the content you will be putting out for that week. Think ahead about the next seven days and the activities or events that you have coming up. Maybe there's a birthday celebration, a baby shower, a holiday, or a short trip planned. Perhaps it is just the week you pay your bills, work in your garden and try out new recipes. Once you have a fairly firm grasp of the week ahead, you can begin to create content. Let your life and everyday activities spark ideas for the content you are putting out. Remember these three categories you want to post under: know, like, and trust. Choose your topic and the way you want to share it and get to posting.

A LOT ALIKE

Failure only exists when you quit chasing your dreams.

9
FAILURE HAS FOOLED US ALL

I can remember how scared I was to step out on my own as an entrepreneur. I had dreamed of being my own boss for most of my life but I was always afraid that I would drop the ball or mess something up if I had too much responsibility. I didn't even think that I had enough value to give someone, let alone enough to charge someone for it. And in all fairness, growing up I didn't have an example of an entrepreneur in my family. I did however, have an example of what consistency and hard work could get you. My mother was a public-school teacher for thirty-three years and my granny worked at a plant for twenty-two years. They were the prime example of how rewarding consistency can be. I never wanted for much.

We All Have Value

The truth of the matter is that there isn't anything that I can share with you that you can't Google or YouTube on your own. This simple truth proves that point that people don't always pay for what you do, they pay for why you do it, as Simon Sinek explained in his book, *Start With Why*. People pay for convenience. Thinking back on it now, I laugh at how afraid I was to share information that I felt like people could easily obtain. But then I realized what people truly needed was my energy more than they needed my knowledge. My delivery and my presentation are what people would ultimately pay for. I wish someone had told me this simple truth a long time ago. Had someone shifted my perspective sooner I would have jumped years sooner. People want to pay you for your brand and the way your brand makes them feel. And that's it. It is that simple. People will pay for who you are and all you have to do is show up and put in the work to provide a brand and service worth paying for. Position yourself as their source of choice.

Is Failure Really a Thing?

I learned a lot of lessons during my first year as a full-time entrepreneur. And one of my biggest lessons was in the department of failing. Not that I experienced a lot of it but after listening to so many entrepreneurs share their journeys, I've learned what it really means to fail. I have always found it so fascinating to analyze the fear we put into things that can't physically harm us. Like getting our feelings hurt or "failing" at a task or goal. I want to challenge how you define failure.

When I was about eight months into my journey, I started hosting branding workshops as a way to expand my brand and footprint, and as a way to further establish myself as an expert in my field. I also wanted to test my market to see how receptive they were to these types of workshops. It took a little work and nudging but a comfortable amount of people did finally sign up for the first one. This gave me hope for future workshops. Now you can imagine that by the second one my confidence was high. I had my graphics guy create my flyer and when I received it, I was extra lit because it looked amazing. Colors were popping and my picture was glowing. I could not wait to drop it and watch the RSVPs roll in. I dropped the flyer on social media, did my social media promoting, and waited. And I waited. Nobody signed up.

Nobody. So, I said, okay, let me do a giveaway. This will get the people going. I proceeded to publicly give away a spot at the workshop. I congratulated the winner with posts and she even reposted it to her page hyping it up even more. And again, I waited. Nothing. Nobody signed up.

Now I'm not going to pretend like my pride wasn't hurt because it was, but I didn't dwell there long. I picked my feelings up off the floor and I said, "Okay, let me figure out why this time didn't work and how I can come back and do it differently."

Failure is simply the world's way of telling you to figure something out. Try something else. Failure only exists when you quit chasing your dreams.

It doesn't exist when things don't go as planned or the people don't show up for your event. Failure isn't found in the box of unsold products at your house. Failure only happens when you stop trying.

How can the F word - failure - be defined? It is the active decision to give up and decide to not figure it out; whatever it is.

Failure only exists when you don't want to find a solution. And as an entrepreneur, one of your main roles is to be a problem solver.

If you are wondering how I solved the empty workshop problem – I figured it out. I looked at the lack of responses as data. What it told me was that some part of my process wasn't resonating with my audience. Maybe it was the price point? Maybe it was the subject line? Could it be that branding was too broad of a topic?

Then I went a step further and I let people complain to help me figure it out even more. That's right, I encouraged my audience to complain so that I could use it as data to solve their problem. Now they had no idea that this was my plan, but the one thing I know about people is that they love to complain. It seems to be the natural thing to do. I once heard Brené Brown say that when we are asked about love, we tell you about heartache. But that's a whole different subject that we can fill up a whole different book on.

The next thing I did was take to my social media page and ask the question, "What's your biggest struggle with social media?" Then I watched as the complaints rolled in. What this told me was that *this* is what people needed help with. I identified the ones I could fix and I took those solutions and made them the focus of my next workshop that was no longer about branding alone, but more focused on social media. My next workshop was a success because I took what seemed like failure and used it to improve my original idea.

I know. It's easier said than done. We have all been paralyzed at the idea of failure at some point or another. But, if you could just shift your perspective to see failure as data instead of seeing it as worth, your life will never be the same again. Learn to take a look at what you are doing that's not working and turn it into numbers and statistics. Check to see if you are serving your target audience or engaging with them the way that is best for them.

In business you may try a strategy, and end up with completely different results than you originally imagined. But don't be discouraged because people are always changing and evolving, which means you should be right there changing and evolving with them.

I once heard someone say, *don't let this process punk you out of your purpose*. I know this whole branding thing can feel overwhelming at times, but remember, you don't have to tell your whole story all at once. Branding is controlled chaos and all you have to do is paint a picture of who you are, one stroke at a time. When you think about painters, they never start with the whole picture on the canvas. They start with one spot of paint and before you know it, the whole picture comes to life. But the process is messy and when they make mistakes (notice I said *when*) they fix it and they keep painting. Adopt this mindset about your brand. Tell your story, one post at a time. Branding is like a controlled chaos. Keep consistently doing the work and trust the process.

Don't Quit!

MY RANDOM FINAL THOUGHTS

One of my favorite questions to ask someone is, "If you could go back and give advice to your younger self, what would you say?" I think this is such a beautiful question because it not only reminds us of how far we have come and the lessons we have learned along the way, but it forces us to look back with grace on all that we have been through. It forces us to be kind to ourselves and acknowledge how far we have come. If you could jump ahead seven years from now, what would you look back and tell yourself to do right now? What would you wish you had done in this moment with your life and your career? Whatever that thing is, decide today to do it.

If I could go back to the moment I decided to quit my job and take a chance in this world as an entrepreneur, I would tell myself two things. First, it would be to make a plan for my mental and emotional health and to make it a priority as if my success depends on it – because it does.

The second thing I would say to myself is that in this world of entrepreneurship, we are all a lot more alike than we are different. Every business in this world, no matter how big or small, has had its fair share of challenges that seem like failures but they all figured them out. So, I would tell myself not to quit.

I hope this book has been an echo of that same message. Don't quit. Learn to reset and restart because while we are alike in many ways, there is only one you and the world needs exactly what you have to offer.

VISUAL MAPPING

The road to social media is paved with purpose, organization and strategy. This next section is dedicated to my note takers and visual friends. Use these pages to make note of what you learned and know to be true about your business. Build a brand you love. Starting here. Starting today.

BRANDING WITH PURPOSE

What was your biggest takeaway from this book?

Think about the different paths your brand can take you. What other goal(s) do you wish to accomplish / results?

_____
_____
_____
_____
_____
_____
_____
_____
_____
_____
_____
_____
_____
_____
_____

What is your unique brand voice?

Branding is how you make people feel through your products and services. What does your brand make people feel? What is your why?

LET'S GET ORGANIZED

Be Able To Explain Why Your Brand Is Important

Business Description / Name / Title:

_____
_____
_____
_____
_____
_____
_____
_____
_____
_____
_____

Mission

_____
_____

Vision

Services/Products

_____
_____
_____
_____
_____
_____
_____
_____
_____

Core Beliefs

_____
_____
_____
_____
_____
_____
_____
_____
_____
_____
_____

WHO IS YOUR PERSON?

How Can I Help You?
If you're talking to everyone then you're talking to no one.

Are they a man or a woman? Age / race? Married or Single? How many children?

_____
_____
_____
_____
_____
_____
_____
_____

What do they do for a living? Introvert, extrovert or ambivert? How do they dress?

_____
_____
_____
_____

_____
_____
_____
_____
_____

How do they spend their free time? Where do they vacation? What type of music do they listen to?

_____
_____
_____
_____
_____
_____
_____
_____

What is the most important thing to them in life? What keeps them up at night? Their fears?

_____
_____
_____
_____

What is their name? Additonal details about them?

ABOUT THE AUTHOR

Maranda Joiner is a native of Jackson, MS. She worked as an on-air hip hop radio personality at 99JAMS WJMI for almost fifteen years. She's also was a TEDx host and has curated and hosted an open mic experience called Synergy Nights for several years. She has consulted and served as the brand manager for talents, placing some on Comedy Central, TruTV and on stage at Essence.

Maranda quit her job to pursue her dream as a brand strategist to help others identify their purpose and feel more connected to the work they do. She helps entrepreneurs, creatives, and business owners find their unique brand voice and connect it to their purpose so they can make money.

REFLECTIONS

REFLECTIONS

REFLECTIONS

REFLECTIONS

REFLECTIONS

REFLECTIONS

www.ingramcontent.com/pod-product-compliance
Lightning Source LLC
Chambersburg PA
CBHW030912080526
44589CB00010B/259